This New Life Together

An Anthology Of Wedding Meditations

CSS Publishing Company, Inc.
Lima, Ohio

Library of Congress Cataloging-in-Publication Data

This new life together : an anthology of wedding meditations.
    p.   cm.
  ISBN 1-55673-597-9
  1. Wedding sermons. 2. Marriage — Sermons. 3. Sermons, American. I. CSS Publishing Company.
BV4278.T47   1994
252'.1—dc20
                          93-43014
                          CIP

ISBN 1-55673-597-9

Table Of Contents

Foreword

Two days after our wedding, a professor of mine, Roger Cooper, sat down and composed a letter to me and my wife. That letter has held a cherished position in our wedding memory book ever since. In that letter he writes:

The impulse which pushes me to compose this letter is the desire to bless you in a special way. God's Word was a part of the wedding ceremony, as the result of pre-planning. It also erupted spontaneously, surprisingly.

I hope that you will hear God's Word in the words you speak with each other. May you find in the words of those who cross your threshold even for an instant, enough strength and encouragement to live by.

May no words tear you from each other. May there always be words by which you are continually reconciled with yourselves, with each other, and with those God gives you as neighbors.

These 20 meditations are rather like that letter. They are composed of words gathered together and grounded in love and concern for those two individuals beginning their new adventure of marriage. On the other hand, they are just words strung together in phrases, sentences and paragraphs. But they have been informed by the Word of God, shared experiences, hopes and dreams.

The authors of these meditations, representing a variety of denominations, have worked closely with many couples making wedding plans. Using simple, but profound words, the authors have constructed thoughts, wishes, stories and blessings designed to inspire, inform and motivate men and women who are working on their relationships with one another and with the Lord. They know that, when used in the wedding ceremony, many of these words may never be heard or appreciated. Standing at the altar, some grooms will be focusing their attention on keeping their knees from knocking together. At the same time there will be brides whose thoughts will have transported them mentally to the reception hall. But in spite of those possibilities, the writers of these meditations know the power of the spoken word. They understand the importance of launching the enterprise of marriage within the context of the Word of God and the family of faith.

Many who pick up this book are pastors looking for bits of inspiration as they work on wedding meditations of their own. Others may use this book as a primer on God's holy design for the wedding partnership. Still others will allow these specially crafted words to minister to them in extraordinary ways as they prepare to minister to others. However you approach this book, may you find a blessing.

Michael L. Thompson
November, 1993

1

Happy Fear

Psalm 128;
Philippians 4:4-7

By John V. Carrier

Today's psalm, which _____ and _____ chose, is both a blessing and an admonition. That is appropriate to a wedding. Everyone present needs to remember what is going on here, as well as wish _____ and _____ well. Why are we here today?

For one thing, we gather to witness their marriage. We come to hear their promises. Maybe someday, as friends and family, we may want to remind them of these vows. And then, maybe we need to rehearse those vows ourselves.

For those of us who are married, these are the promises we made, or ones similar, and it is good for us to hear them again. For those who are not married, they are commitments you may someday utter. At the very least, they are basic to the assurances of marriage that affect all of us in one way or another. Today especially, this is the character of _____ and _____ relationship that they are putting before the entire community. They are going public with their intentions for their life together.

We gather to support that relationship. We are backing you, _____ and _____! We are for you in your marriage. This is very important. We all need support from time to time, and it is especially good to get support for something so important as a marriage.

We also gather to pray. In the presence of God and God's people, we recognize that this joyous occasion is also holy work. God is at work here, bringing two people together and uniting them as one. In that unity there is a vision of life that is Godly.

How is this marriage Godly? That will be up to _____ and _____, and up to us who are a part of their lives, and up to the guidance and power of the Holy Spirit. It all works together. When it does not work together, it does not work at all.

Part of the Godly nature of their life together is some basically religious activity, beginning with this wedding. This is a Christian ceremony, in a Christian setting, not just a romantic ceremony in a sentimental setting. We ask God to be present in this relationship. The scriptures we read tell us of the need for God to be a main ingredient in our life together. God is the source of true joy.

A good portion of the Godliness of this relationship is not classically religious. It is instead, everyday life. _____ and _____, how you live will be informed by what you believe. It is important for you to realize that everything you have, including yourselves and each other, is a gift of God. It is a sign of God's love for you.

Now, hopefully, this will lead you to a life of thanksgiving . . . a life that recognizes that everything about you can and must be turned over to God. In that way, "the peace of God which passes all understanding, will keep your hearts and minds in Christ Jesus."

Why do you want your heart and mind in Christ Jesus? Why do you want the peace of God? Because marriage without it is a drag! Marriages without God fall apart. Why? Because as much as we love each other in our relationships, we will not always agree. We will not always feel very loving toward each other. We will not always enjoy the company of our spouse. There will be times when we will wonder why and how we ever got ourselves in this situation in the first place. We may be tempted to stray or be distracted by other people, jobs, family, friends, recreation, vices, illness . . . all because of sin. We will sin against each other.

8

Now you may never sin against your spouse, but I guarantee you, your spouse will sin against you. Seriously, that is sometimes the way we see it. When things are broken, we place blame, and usually we place it anywhere but on ourselves. But blame does not help. What we need is forgiveness. The love that includes forgiveness is a gift that comes only from God. It is most completely displayed and given through Jesus Christ, and it is the most Godly activity you can bring to a relationship.

When we put Christ into our lives, sin loses its power to destroy us. We see ourselves, as well as others, as sinners who need God in order to live life in peace and joy. We need to love and to be loved, and love is expressed most deeply in our deepest need: to forgive and to be forgiven.

So here we are. The body of Christ, the church, is gathered together to put this marriage in the context of God in Christ Jesus, for there is our peace and there is our joy.

"The peace of God which passes all understanding, keep your hearts and minds in Christ Jesus." Amen.

John V. Carrier is Lutheran campus pastor of Winona State University, Winona, Minnesota.

2
The Solid Rock On Which We Stand!

Matthew 7:24-29

By Robert S. Crilley

_____ and _____: The occasion of any wedding always confronts a preacher with the challenge of finding a middle ground between two extremes. On the one hand, it would seem, down through the years, that everything worth saying about a rich and rewarding relationship has, in some way or another, already been said — most memorably perhaps by the world's poets. On the other hand, the two of you are the only ones who can actually voice what needs to be said here today; and I honestly believe that the true meaning of the love you both share has been expressed far more powerfully by your presence, than could any message I might hope to render.

That challenge, however, is easily overcome by the pleasure, privilege, and personal honor I now feel, and indeed continue to find, in being allowed to speak a word to the two of you on this special day. As I am sure you will agree, this is a day that both of you have spent a lot of time talking about, thinking about, dreaming about, planning about — maybe even worrying about just a little. And at long last, it has finally arrived!

Your family and friends, of course, have all gathered together to share this day with you. We have come because we love you, and because we recognize that the two of you love each other very, very much. But we have come here to this place of worship, because there is another love we wish to witness as well — the love of God. I believe that it is God's love which has led you to this place; and it is our common hope and prayer that it shall be God's love which will follow you from this place, and continue to abide with you both in all places that you shall enjoy and experience together.

Today the two of you begin building a new life as husband and wife; but before you actually get started, I want to take a moment and invite you to consider the days ahead. I realize, of course, that that's not always the easiest thing to do. The great baseball pundit Yogi Berra, when asked by a reporter about his team's chances for a pennant, once quipped, "I never make predictions — especially about the future!"

And yet, it seems to me that we are safely able to predict some things in life, because they are inevitable. It doesn't matter who you are, where you live, or what you do. It makes no difference how powerful, how popular, or how prominent you've become. One's accumulated wealth or wisdom is of little significance, for some truths are so tightly woven into the fabric of human existence that they simply establish themselves as unalterable and absolute. You could whisper them as easily to the sleeping child during a lullaby, as you could along a quiet corridor of the nursing home. Because, like it or not, life carries with it some certainties which each and every one of us will experience ... sooner or later.

It might very well be that Benjamin Franklin was thinking something along these same lines, when he first penned the now well-known phrase, "... in this life nothing is certain but death and taxes." Those are two. I would like to add to the list a third: change.

Of course, that may strike both of you as being so obvious that it hardly needs mentioning. Still, the unavoidable fact is that nothing, at least in this life, remains constant for very long. Seasons come and go, nations rise and fall, and the pendulum of cultural values seems to swing back and forth from generation to generation. Try as one might, you can never step twice into the same river ... for that which once was, no longer is, nor shall it really ever be again. And I am probably not alone in the belief that to live is to experience change.

Now, the two of you may not fully understand, nor yet be able to appreciate it completely, but from this very moment on, your lives have also changed. Of course, in many respects, it is a welcomed change, and no doubt, one well received by you both. Still, because this is an occasion marked by change, I have chosen as today's scripture lesson a brief passage from the seventh chapter of the gospel of Matthew.

Admittedly, this parable may seem a rather strange text for a wedding sermon. However, even though one's marriage might be made in heaven, it remains a partnership to be worked out here on earth. Like these two builders, the two of you will want to choose carefully that upon which your life together will be founded. Such, at least, was my original purpose in selecting this passage, because I had always believed that the fundamental difference between the wise builder and the foolish builder was where each decided to construct his house — one on rock, the other on sand.

In fact, for the longest time, I was persuaded that that was indeed the only difference. After all, there's no indication in the text that one house was larger than the other, or even more expensive. Matthew makes no mention of one being thrown together rather hastily, while the other took years of skillful planning. There are no soil samples taken, no environmental impact studies pursued, no insurance policies signed. The only difference recorded here is not so much in how these houses were built, but in where.

However, I am beginning to wonder whether there is something even more significant which separates these two builders. True enough, their houses differ in terms of location, but what makes one wise and the other foolish is not merely their choice of real estate. That's part of it, to be sure, but I believe that there may be yet another striking contrast.

The more I study this parable, the more I am persuaded that what actually distinguishes wise from foolish is that one anticipated that the weather might someday change and the other did not. Because if you think about it, in this parable, if the storms never come ... both houses remain sturdy and standing. In fact, from an architectural standpoint, there is no liability in building one's structure upon sand, if the storms don't ever come. Ah, but the storms do come — just as they always will — and what really separates these two is that one realized that indeed someday they would.

No doubt, both of these home owners began construction when the heavens were a canopy of clear blue, and the warm days gently laid a soft shoulder of sunlight against the landscape. However, only one was wise enough to recognize that the skies can never remain calm and cloudless. And so, one wisely built upon that which would not change!

_____ and _____, today you are setting the cornerstone for the new life which you will both continue to build together. As on this day, there will be times when your house is filled with the sweet music of joy and laughter; but there will also be occasions when the only sounds are the hushed and trembling whispers of pain or sorrow. There will be bright afternoons when warm sunlight shines through every window; but there will also be evenings when the shadows lengthen and the rooms grow dark and cold. There will be festive occasions when all of your family and friends crowd around the table in celebration; but there will also be lonely times when the very place you call home seems suddenly empty and strangely unfamiliar.

Inevitably, there will be such times for you both. The storms will roll in eventually, because the weather — just like every other aspect of life — is always subject to change. As did the wise man in this parable, I want to encourage the two of you to build your marriage upon a foundation that will not change and cannot cease — the love of God. And toward that goal, I want to share with you now a very simple truth. If you like, you may scribble it down in the corner of the blueprints, and ponder upon it later, as you draw up the floor plans of life you will soon begin building.

The truth is this: Love does not consist only in looking at one another. Sometimes love means looking in the same direction. What that direction will be, I leave now to the two of you. But know this: If you are looking together, you will find it. And you will realize that which you dream together ... possess that which you hope together ... conquer that which you battle together ... and learn that which you live together. Because you do so together with God.

_____ and _____, don't ever forget that God is part of this union as well. The life you begin building this day, you begin building with God; and when finally the construction is complete, God will be there as surely as God is now here. God's love will see you both that far, because God's love has already seen you this far. Such is the nature of love — especially God's love — a love which will not change and cannot cease. And what's more, you can build on it!

Robert S. Crilley is pastor of First Presbyterian Church of Grapevine, Texas.

3
Wedding Admonition

By Paul L. Sandin

_____ and _____, the marriage vows that you have exchanged today are voluntary and equal, the same for the man as for the woman. Regard them not as burdens to weigh you down, but as winged hopes and promises to bear you up into a more happy and abundant life.

Remember, true love is not the passion to possess or to rule, but the desire to give and to bless. Let no secrets divide you, no jealousies come between you, no differences bring bitterness in your hearts. Remember that in true love, your sorrows are cut in half, and your joys are doubled because you share them together. I charge you, don't be motivated by prosperity, nor overcome by adversity; but seek to find fulfillment through a firm faith in God and in each other.

As you make your home together may it indeed be a place of happiness and contentment for yourselves. But may it also be a place where your families and friends may come and find love, joy and peace. But even more than these, may that home be the place from which you go forth each day to be a blessing to all with whom you come in daily contact.

The God of Love unites you together as husband and wife. Go now in peace, trusting that the love which unites you today in holy marriage will also make you one forever.

**Appropriate place for special music or Lord's Prayer.

Paul L. Sandin is pastor of First Baptist Church, Patterson, New Jersey.

4
Wedding Prayer

By Kenneth E. Crouch

After the prayer of invocation:

You look so beautiful and so handsome — like any prince and princess! We remember the fairytales of our childhood where the prince and princess were married and lived happily ever after. Since that does not happen today, I am obligated to instruct you. No activity is entered into so joyfully and with such high expectations as is marriage. But the happiness does not come automatically. You are not entering a partnership where each partner is asked to give 50 percent; rather you are entering a union where you may give 70 percent or 90 percent or even 100 percent. Listen to these words of scripture: may they inspire you as you enter a new way of loving and living (usually parts of 1 Corinthians 13 follow).

A wedding prayer

Eternal God, who has willed the estate of marriage and who has taught us the way of love, we ask that you would bless this marriage. Give to _____ and _____ the desire and the ability to keep the vows that they have made. Where selfishness would show itself, give an extra measure of love; where mistrust is a temptation, give confidence; where misunderstanding intrudes, give gentleness and patience. Give to them many times of joy and peace and happiness as their love for each other deepens. May their home be visited frequently by laughter and pleasant surprises and dear friends. Teach them the values of listening and giving and saying the kind word. Give them strength to endure the bitter moments that life may put in their way. Make strong their faith and their hope when they have to face problems that seem too big. May they long remember the exciting days of their courtship; may tender affection always be a part of their love for each other. Let them know that you are with them and that you care for them when the night seems darkest. We pray this in the Spirit of the Christ who taught us to pray, Our Father ... Amen.

Kenneth E. Crouch is minister of Casas Adobes Congregational (UCC), Tucson, Arizona.

5
Joyful Are Those Who Receive God's Love

Matthew 5:1-12

By Paul Lintern

Blessed are those who know that without God they are in-
    complete
theirs is the kingdom of heaven.
This passage is a poem,
a teaching by Jesus which "covers the bases" of life.
In the beatitudes, as the second passage is called,
Jesus is describing the nature of being in tune with God's love,
Most translations use the word blessed, some use the word
    happy,
and while both are legitimate,
I think the most appropriate translation is
joyful — I am filled with that which makes my heart leap;
a wholeness, a peace, a completeness,
and sense that this is right,
and while it will very often bring happiness,
it is not completely tied to that emotion that says,
I've got no troubles; everything's fine.
To be full of joy is to recognize God's place in the midst of
all things — relationships, household, job,
accomplishments, failures, arguments,
frustrations, possessions, confusion.
To know, when things are not under control
that we do belong to the one who
ultimately is in control,
and that our Creator, through Jesus has made us one.

_____ and _____, in your relationship, it is that joy
that will sustain you,
That will give you purpose when obstacles with job and money
and goals overwhelm you.
That will give you the courage and determination to fight for
reconciliation, when conflicts arise,
That will give you the vision to see the life that you are building
together and the hope that is found
in the love of God through Jesus.
Joyful are those who mourn because they have had the courage
to love,
they shall be comforted and assured that it was worth it.
Joyful are those who humbly accept what God has given them,
they shall have everything they could want.
Joyful are those who hunger and thirst to do that which God
would
want them to do — they shall be fed.
Joyful are the merciful, the forgiving, for mercy and forgiveness shall return to them.
Joyful are those who understand that God is present and loving in all things,
they shall see God active in their lives.
Joyful are those who work for ways which build wholeness
and peace
in the world and in the home — they shall be called children
of God.
Joyful are you when others do not understand your motiva-
tion for love and forgiveness,
and you are hurt because of it; God understands and is with
you always.

And joyful are you, _____ and _____, as you allow the joy of love through Jesus
to prevail in your marriage. Amen.

*Paul Lintern is associate pastor of First Lutheran Church,
Mansfield, Ohio.*

6
Your Gifts To Each Other

Ephesians 5:33

By Ronald K. Brooks

I love weddings! I love everything about them. I enjoy the counselling with new couples, the wedding rehearsal, the joy and the love that fills a sanctuary during a wedding service. I enjoy the pomp and circumstance of the wedding service, but most of all I think I like the wedding reception best, and one part in particular — the opening of the wedding gifts. I love watching the faces of this new couple as they unwrap the gifts. Big and small each carries a message of love and hope for the new couple. And I can't think about wedding gifts without remembering a story shared with me about Grandma's gift to the new young couple.

The honeymoon is over. The groom had left for work when there was a knock at the door. The young bride opened the door to discover Grandma's aged but friendly face. With a smile she announced, "I am bringing you a wedding present."

But instead of offering the young woman a package, the elderly woman stepped into the house and said: "Come on. I want to show you how to make an apple pie." Now you need to understand that Grandma's apple pie was heavenly. She had a way to make a pie crust that was so light and flaky it practically floated, and she added some secret ingredient to the filling (that she would never reveal) that made her apple pies melt in your mouth. The young bride could barely believe that Grandma was showing her how to make her extra-special apple pie. It took some time to get the job done but finally she learned all of Grandma's secrets.

"Now," said the older woman, "I want you to iron one of your husband's shirts." The poor bride had to iron the same shirt six times before the elderly woman was satisfied. But finally she got it. Grandma prepared to leave. The bride, not understanding, said, "But where is my present, Grandma?" The old lady laughed: "Why, _____, I have been giving it to you all morning."

_____ and _____ you will receive many gifts today, but the most important gifts you will receive will not come in wrapping paper. You see, Grandma understood that the most important gifts given in a marriage are the ones given after the honeymoon has ended, the day-to-day gifts of sharing a life together. Oh, certainly Grandma's gift had an old-fashioned flavor to it but there are certain gifts that you can only give to one another . . . and they will make or break your marriage.

Ephesians 5:33 says, "Husbands love your wives as yourself, and wives respect your husbands." Give to one another the gift of respect. Respect one another's opinions. Honor one another's emotional highs and lows. Support one another. Encourage each other. Cherish one another's company and above all love one another as you love yourself. Give these gifts to one another daily and your marriage will be blessed. Amen.

Ronald K. Brooks is pastor of the Lawrence United Methodist Church, Lawrence, Michigan.

7
A Couple Who Do Feet

By Jim Heinemeier

(Adapted from imagery created by Harry Wendt of Crossways International)

This is kind of personal, but ...
> how are your feet doing?
>> I'll bet they're hot and tired and achy.

Wouldn't it feel great if right about now all of us could kick off our shoes and some nice person would be there to rub those hot, tired, achy feet!

I'd like to talk to you about your feet.
> About taking care of your feet.
>> (Yes, I know. This is a wedding!)

I'd like to talk about couples who do feet.
> In the hope the two of you will become a couple who does feet.

A long time ago
> (before shoes and before sidewalks)
>> people going from here to there would end up with dusty, hot, tired feet —
>>> and perhaps (since they shared the path with animals of all sorts)
>>>> with fragrant feet!

If the travelers were fortunate enough to be guests at someone's home after their long walk, it was customary for the
thoughtful host to have his servant wash his guests' feet.

Or his wife could do it!

We've come a long way!

(or have we?)

The night Jesus was betrayed and arrested he and his fearless
band of followers were eating together.

It was his last supper.

The disciples of Jesus had been arguing along the way as to
which of the 12 of them was the greatest,

It ended up a 12-way tie!

So, their feet are hot and tired and dusty.

There are no servants around.

There are no wives around.

It's easy to picture no one volunteering to wash the feet of
the other.

No one was willing to bend down and be the servant.
The atmosphere was thick with arrogance and one-up-manship.

(Sort of like a lot of marriages we know, right?)

To break the spell — and to teach them and you and all of
us a powerfully important lesson, Jesus got up from the table, took off his jacket, tied a towel around his waist, knelt
down and proceeded to become the servant —

he washed his disciples' feet!

When he was done, he said, "Do you know what I have done
for you? If I your Lord and teacher have washed your feet,
you ought to wash one another's feet. I have set an example
for you, that you should do as I have done!"

Some have called this the "neglected" sacrament. In many churches, foot-washing still happens "on the night Jesus was betrayed." As a matter of fact, I did it myself a few nights ago for a couple of highly embarrassed first communion class members!

Jesus — and I — are talking about serving one another.
　About being humble enough,
　　giving enough,
　　self-sacrificing enough,
　　　and, yes, strong enough,
　　　　to serve one another.
Even — especially — in ways that are unpleasant.

We all know too many marriages where there's no way either partner is about to serve the other. Those marriages are as close to pure hell as it gets.

And we all know too many marriages where one serves the other
　— but is not served in return
　　One partner says, "You are here to serve me, and all my needs!"
　　　And the other is just unhealthy enough to go
　　　　along with it.

All of us here today are praying that the marriage the two of you will create will be one where each washes the feet of the other.
　Where each serves the other.
　Where each seeks diligently what is best for the other.
　Where each is unable to do enough for the other.

Something very strong and basic deep inside you is going to rebel against all this, unless ...
　unless you stay very, very close to the One whose foot-washing ways you will need to imitate.

If you stay very close to Jesus Christ and his loving,
serving,
self-sacrificing,
foot-washing life for you and for all humankind,
then you, _____, will become a husband who does feet,
and you, _____, will become a wife who does feet
and you, _____ and _____ will become a couple who does feet.

It will feel so good!
And all the world will know that the two of you are his people because of your foot-washing love for each other.

In the name of the One who shows us how to do feet! Amen.

Jim Heinemeier is pastor of Lutheran Church of the Good Shepherd, Reno, Nevada.

8
Dressing For The Marriage

For A Protestant-Catholic Marriage

Colossians 3:12-17

By Mary Venema Swierenga

Well. Here you are, finally, _____ and _____, all dressed in your wedding clothes: a lovely, lovely bridal gown and a dashing GQ wedding tuxedo. You are a very attractive couple on this most significant day of your lives, a couple I like very much — each of you separately, and as a couple. Behind my affection for you is my respect: you each have deep spiritual convictions which have shaped your character as Christian young adults. You've done a lot of work with me, with Father _____, with the _____ Conference to prepare yourselves spiritually and emotionally for being married. We've talked very honestly about marriage in our premarital counseling sessions. I believe you're more than ready to joyfully undertake the challenges of marriage. Right now, fitted out in all your wedding finery, you're undoubtedly agreeing with me 100 percent!

Now, I don't want to be misunderstood here, but I have a question to ask. When you take off your wedding clothes, what are you going to put on? When you take off the bridal gown and the tux, what do you put on for the marriage? How does one dress for success in a marriage? What are you going to wear to ensure that yours will be enduring and satisfying?

Paul, in Colossians 3:12-17, has some suggestions for a marriage wardrobe. First, put on compassion. This is something you wear inside. It has to do with having a heart for the other, each of you having the other at heart. Literally, compassion means "a heart of pity." Compassion is an inner attitude you each have toward the other — an inner stance you each take — a fullness of tender caring for and about the other's vulnerability and strengths which will overflow into how you treat each other privately and in public. Compassion is an inner garment.

On top of compassion, put on kindness. Now there's an article of clothing that you get to be in short supply in a marriage sometimes! After a while, you really get to know the other's weaknesses and sore spots. Kindness doesn't sweep these under the rug when they are destructive to the marriage, but when you are clothed with kindness you will be seeking the other's good as you deal with the weaknesses and sore spots. Kindness is a garment with healing in its wings.

Then there's another item of clothing that does a marriage good: humility. If ever there is an arena where pride and the need to be right and the struggle for power occur, it's in a marriage. Lack of humility leads to every kind of struggle, whether it's a struggle for power over the checking account, over the kids, over whose turn it is to make sure you don't run out of milk and orange juice, or a power struggle over who was supposed to be home when to do what. Humility is far from abject submission to the other's whims and wants. Rather, humility recognizes the other's equal status, recognizes that each has needs and plans which are equally valid. You can only put on humility when you remember that each of you is not God but an equal-in-God's-eyes child of God.

Gentleness is another worthy garment for a marriage. Aristotle has defined gentleness as the mean between too much anger and not enough. Gentleness has strength in it, but it is not the strength of the self-controlled person. Gentleness is the garment of the God-controlled person. Gentleness has sweetness in it, too. When you put on gentleness, the other can take off self-defensive armor, wariness, fearfulness, and can put on trust. Every marriage could use several garments of gentleness.

Now, here's an absolutely necessary article of clothing for a marriage: patience. Each of you will discover, if you haven't already, that the other has the capacity to drive you crazy! Whether it's chewing ice cubes, or trying to ignore for a week, already, that stack of magazines that the other has set out on the table to read but hasn't gotten to yet, or switching channels constantly with the all-powerful remote control, or never allowing enough time to arrive on time — it doesn't matter what the issue is: marriage takes patience. And these are just the surface things. Patience requires humor, a spirit of live and let live. But mostly patience takes love. Because patience is required for coping with the other's emotional habits, with the other's incomprehensible-to-you enjoyments, with the other's weaknesses.

Another essential garment for a marriage is a spirit of forbearance and forgiveness. There's a lot that needs to be endured in a marriage, a lot that requires forbearance. It is a spirit of forgiveness that makes difficult things endurable, maybe even erases them. I could never comprehend the movie *The Love Story* which ended with the line, "Love means never having to say you're sorry." Nowhere more than in marriage, love is repeatedly having to say "I'm sorry." Don't say it to get out of a tight spot. Say it because you know that in no other relationship is the other so vulnerable, so easily hurt. And when the other has asked forgiveness, grant it. Speak not only your pain, but speak the word of peace as well.

If compassion is marriage's inner, attitudinal, garment, and if kindness, humility, gentleness, patience, forbearance and forgiveness are its active-wear shirts and pants and skirts and socks, then love is the overcoat. "On top of all these things," Paul says, "put on love." Love keeps a marriage warm.

Love is not an emotion. Oh, it is maybe a little, partly, that. But love as an emotion can wear thin and threadbare when feelings ebb. Love as the overcoat that keeps a marriage warm is made up of two things, both of which must be there for marriage to endure: commitment and caring. I'd describe commitment the way a college professor of mine did: commitment is a small island of certainty. It's an island you create for each other. It's the solid ground on which your marriage rests. "I will be there for you." That's the commitment you make with your vows. But what good is commitment without caring? Caring says, "I commit myself to you. I will be there for you."

When you marry, you signal, in a real way, the end to your own rugged individualism, your own unfettered freedom, your control over your own life. Now marriage does not mean that you lose your individualism or your freedom or your responsibility to control your life. It does mean that the other will now always be a factor that conditions your decision making. When you marry, you commit yourself to the other, you bind yourself with promises to love the other as yourself, you promise to caringly bring your whole self to your relationship. Wear that caring, committed love you've promised today as the overcoat that will keep you warm for a lifetime together.

There is one more thing that needs to be said — actually, what I'm about to say undergirds everything I've said to far. These clothes Paul invites us to put on are not made of natural fibers. They are woven of spiritual stuff. These are supernatural clothes, and only those who have the Spirit of Jesus Christ can really put them on. Try as you might in your own power to create them, they run counter to our human nature. For instance, human nature says, "I'll do my fair share but no more." Or, "She deserved it." Or "It's his turn to give in." Compassion, humility, kindness, gentleness, forgiveness, love — these don't come naturally. They are gifts God gives us when we pray for them.

_____ and _____, earlier I commended you for your deep spiritual Christian characters. I would invite you, from this very first day to ground your marriage in a life of prayer for each other, but, more importantly, with each other. Together pray daily to be clothed in spiritual garments so that tonight when you take off your beautiful wedding garments, you can begin to put on the spiritual garments which will keep your marriage warm for years and years and years.

Put on then, as God's chosen ones, holy and beloved compassion, kindness, lowliness, meekness, and patience, forbearing one another and, if one has a complaint against another, forgiving each other; as the Lord has forgiven you, so you must also forgive. And above all these things, put on love, which binds everything in perfect harmony. Let the peace of Christ rule in your hearts.
— Colossians 3:12-15a

For this word from God's Word, thanks be to God! Amen.

Mary Venema Swierenga is associate pastor of Vienna Presbyterian Church, Vienna, Virginia.

9
From Two To One

By B. David Hostetter

(May be read when the marriage candle is lit from two individual or family candles.)

From the duality: male and female
Made in likeness to God who is one ...
From the polarities: father and mother:
Individualities: daughter or son ...

From the convergence of seeds in the womb
Birth brings emergence of our personhood ...
From singularity: "I" comes to be
In the plurality of family ...

From the possessiveness of what is mine
To the sharing of all that is ours ...
From the past and our separate ways
On to tomorrow our one wedded path ...

Lighting the candle for new unity
Being ourselves though in one harmony.
Crossing the gulf between heaven and earth
Christ makes At-ONE-ment with God by our faith.

B. David Hostetter is a retired Presbyterian pastor in Wolcott, New York.

10
Marriage: Endearing And Enduring

For A Medical Student

By Charles R. Leary

Life has a way of challenging us with new beginnings. Some are well planned like this marriage. But many are unplanned, even unpredictable, like an illness, a forced job change or any other unpredictable thing that requires major adjustments. But in all cases new beginnings provide us the occasion to assess and reassess where we are in life. We are here today celebrating a beginning for _____ and _____. The bride and groom will pardon me if I sound a bit crude, but it may just feel like an ending to them. They have made it distinctly clear to me that they have been "waiting" for this for seven years or longer.

Call it what you will, what we do right now marks the end of a preparation which was marked by friendship and suspense, courtship and planning, waiting and longing. It becomes the "rite of passage" into what we call marriage, and, believe me, that will have no less of the same elements of friendship and suspense, courtship and planning, waiting and longing, and a catalogue of other ingredients that can produce growth if handled rightly. It can produce death if handled improperly.

_____ and _____, I am happy to tell you that you have provided each one of us a grand and colorful opportunity to assess our own status in life. This occasion enables each of us to evaluate where we have been in life and where we are going. And it matters not whether we are married or single, young or old, employed or unemployed, this occasion enables us to focus on those positive values that build character and the ingredients that make intimate personal relationships endearing and enduring.

The first thing we look for in a healthy marriage is some kind of equality of sharing. And when I say sharing, I don't mean a 50-50 deal. I don't even mean a 100-100 deal. I am thinking of a relationship where each of you make a 60-40 commitment. You give 60 percent and expect 40 percent. When each does that, you'll end up with an overlap of commitment, a healthy merging of interests and enthusiasm which cuts through the barriers and conflicts that can occur in such an intimate bonding.

Another ingredient for a healthy marriage involves how to keep the individuality that makes you who you are. Some conclude that once they are married all they need is each other. Sounds good. Feels good for a while.

"Variety is the spice of life," though. We assume you will do a variety of things together. What I am going to say may sound strange, but just for a moment. I ask you to think of a boxing ring. I am sure you have already guessed, if you didn't already know, that I am not a boxer. But it's like this: if you are going to be skillful at anything — medicine, management, computers, flying, boxing, nursing, music, art, sports, gardening, and yes, being a person — whatever it may be — you have your own practice room. And so I ask you to picture in your mind a boxing ring.

_____, you must have your own practice room. It is your room. _____ cannot get into your room. You can bring other persons into your room with you but she cannot enter it. This is where you do all kinds of things affirming and being affirmed. You have exchanges with others that enrich your life and affirm your identity.

And then, _____, you have your practice room. It is all yours. _____ cannot get into your room. But you can invite others into it. In your room you do the things that make you feel good about yourself and give you a sense of personal identity and security. It enriches your life.

Then in the middle, _____ and _____ have their own practice room, twice the size of the other rooms. In this larger room is where you share your lives together. What goes on here is your business, and nobody else's. Here is where you will share all your intimacies. Much of it will be joyful. We have to promise you, however, that some of it will be painful. Have you ever seen a rose garden that has no weeds or thorns? I am sure you hope, and we all hope with you, that your garden can be handled in such a way as to nurture and build a relationship that is endearing and enduring, capable of adjusting to the changes life will bring.

Let me extend this boxing ring analogy a bit. If you only have the center ring, and not your private practice rooms too — never have interests apart from each other — then you stand the chance, a very big chance, that this thing we call marriage can fast become boring and routine and familiar. The psychologists say it this way: you have to keep resistance alive in a healthy and growing relationship.

Finally, how can I talk about what we call trust without sounding parental? It's just the way it is: you have to be able to trust each other to go into his or her own private practice room, or boxing ring, for that is where each of you will continually be enriched and enabled to bring back to the center ring, some freshness, some variety, and some real unearned charm. We don't want to see you cloning each other.

If there is ever an inkling of a problem, consider it an SOS signal. Don't let an SOS threaten a vital relationship. The moment an SOS signal appears, begin a process of triage. Get all the help needed. "Nip it in the bud," and it won't become malignant.

We are about to let it begin. In support of your wish to make all your dreams come true, I hereby ask you to turn toward each other, join your right hands, look each other in the eye, and make your vows.

Charles R. Leary is a retired Episcopal clergyman in Medway, Ohio.

11

Three Building Blocks To A Happy Marriage

By Trevor Herm

I'd like to take a few moments to reflect on our scripture, as we think about the building blocks to a happy marriage: faith, hope, and love. All of us who are married would do well to think on these things.

First of all, faith, in God. I know that God plays an important part in each of your lives. It was God who brought you together, and it is God who will keep you together, even through the struggles that every marriage has. And so we make God a part of this service as you dedicate yourselves to each other, you are also publicly acknowledging God's presence in your lives, and inviting him to be a part of this commitment you are about to make. And I'm sure God will bless your marriage, because you've asked for his help.

And then we need to have faith in each other. As we see God's faithfulness to us, that helps us to keep our faith in each other strong. There are bound to be times when we let each other down, but if we can keep our faith in the other person, our faith can help to build them back up.

The second building block is hope. Hope is similar to faith, but when we go through the difficult times we are sure to face in marriage, and it's difficult, to anticipate now what struggles may lie ahead, it's hope that will allow us to be able to see the rainbow at the end of the storm, the light at the end of the tunnel. While our faith keeps our commitment intact, it's hope that keeps our spirits up when life tries to get us down. Hope will help us to see good even in the midst of the bad, and hope will keep us hanging in there until things get better. The hope we are talking about is not an iffy hope, like hoping we win the lottery, but a sure and solid hope based on our faith in God.

The third building block is love, the greatest of the three. Think for a moment of the love you feel for each other right now, and know that that love is real. But it's more than a feeling that you bring to this commitment of marriage. We bring all that we have, all that we are, and we give it in love. Jesus' love led him to die for us, and your love for each other will lead you to give sacrificially to each other.

May your new life today bring all the happiness that you feel today, and may faith and hope become the building blocks for true love to grow in your lives, and in all of our lives.

Trevor Herm is pastor of Yale and Greenwood United Methodist churches, Yale, Michigan.

12

Love Is A Many Splendored Thing

Song Of Solomon 8:6-7
Psalm 100
1 Corinthians 13

by John C. Bush

Some of us here today will remember The Four Aces, a popular singing group from the mid 1950s, and their hit recording of "Love Is A Many Splendored Thing." Indeed, love is a many splendored thing — a truth celebrated and attested to us by the special fascination of weddings, with their wonderful music, bright smiles and all those new or rented clothes.

But that is only the half of it. Love also is a many splintered thing. It is one of the two most basic human emotions, the other of which is hate, according to some understandings of psychology. Both emotions are always present in every human relationship.

If these elements are so important to human personality and to the ways we relate to one another, then surely one of life's major challenges is to learn to deal creatively with the sense of ambivalence they represent. Life's contrary emotions remind us that at every point of decision, at every moment of commitment, we are choosing among alternatives. Saying "yes" to this one means saying "no" to a whole array of others. Today we are here to witness the "yes" being said to each other by _____ and _____.

The writer of the Song of Solomon, one of the most beautiful and erotic love poems ever written, says of love: "Its flashes are flashes of fire." Which is another way of saying that love is both a many splendored thing and a many splintered one as well. It is life's most enduring and rewarding emotion. It is also its most dangerous.

The Greek language in which the New Testament is primarily written knows three words which are rendered as "love" in English, and each word has a specific and special meaning. One of these words, the one used most often by New Testament writers is *agape*. This is a selfless love, unmotivated by such factors as beauty or worth. It describes God's love for us, because God loves us not because of what we might do for God, not because of our beauty or goodness, but only because God is love. We cannot return such love in kind; we respond to it only with faith — acceptance, commitment — giving ourselves over to the God who loves us so. We celebrate that in this service today, too.

Another of the words for love, and one which the New Testament never uses, is *eros*, from which comes our word "erotic." This is sexual love, a vital healthy part of what it means to be human. As people of faith who are also sexual beings, we celebrate that today, as well.

The third word, *philao*, means filial love, the love of husband and wife, of parents and children, of deep and abiding friends. It partakes of portions of each of the other concepts, and does honor to the genuine humanity of those who share it and to the spiritual and physical bond that unites them.

It is this love — their love for each other and the love God has for them — that we celebrate with _____ and _____ today in this public recognition of their special personal and spiritual relationship, and which is the key to a Christian understanding of love and marriage. It provides for the creative expression and fulfillment of our human personalities and potential. It has room for give-and-take; it allows for the existence, the acceptance, and sometimes even the settling, of differences by way of affectionate understanding and reasonableness.

Which is not to say that in love all differences between a wife and husband will be settled. There are some differences in every human relationship which simply must be accepted and lived with. Marriage is far too complex a relationship to expect unanimity. G. K. Chesterton once observed that he had seen many happy marriages, but never a compatible one. Even so, Christian marriage brings to this relationship, to this "yes" said between two distinct individuals, that element of spiritual commitment which we intend "till death do us part." It is this intentional spiritual bond that lends a sense of permanence, and therefore its own special form of freedom and trust, to the marriage relationships.

So, in this context, hear again the words of Paul, this time as they are expressed in paraphrase by J. B. Phillips:

> "This love of which I speak is slow to lose patience — it looks for a way of being constructive. It is not possessive: it is neither anxious to impress nor does it cherish inflated ideas of its own importance.
>
> "Love has good manners and does not pursue selfish advantage. It is not touchy. It does not keep account of evil or gloat over the wickedness of other people. On the contrary, it is glad with all . . . when truth prevails.
>
> "Love knows no limit to its endurance, no end to its trust, no fading of its hope; it can outlast anything. It is, in fact, the one thing that still stands when all else has fallen."

John C. Bush is pastor of Grace Presbyterian Church, Madison, Alabama.

13

The First Marriage

Genesis 2:18-24

By James McKarns

In the midst of a strange and beautiful world, the first man stood in awe, looking about at the new creation. Everything was most lovely but a feeling of loneliness lingered within him.

He saw the heavens with their floating clouds and flying birds. He viewed the virgin earth, displaying its mountains, lakes, trees, flowers and many animals. He was fascinated and happy but still knew he was not totally complete. Then he saw a woman, for the first time and shouted in joy that he had found someone similar to himself. She too had been feeling lonely and they ran to meet each other and embraced. Then both felt very happy and complete. They were no longer strangers in paradise. That's one version of the story we read in Genesis — the oldest book of the Bible.

The Bible points out this was all arranged according to God's own personal plan. Until this meeting took place, creation was not complete and God was still at work. Now the divine plan of God was all in order. God saw it was very good and rested.

The exact time and manner in which these events occurred, we don't know. But we do know these same types of wonderful meetings between men and women have continued ever since. They happen every day, all over the world.

It is that original love, created by God, which has brought this couple (_____ and _____) to the altar today. They have discovered each other, shared their histories and dreams, looked into each other's eyes, embraced in tenderness and said, "I love you." Thus every wedding takes us back to paradise, where it all began.

Today they (_____ and _____) will vow their life-long promises to share their lives. Like that original union, this one, too, is a most happy occasion of a new beginning, a complete trust and an outward expression of a deep inner love.

We smile with a sense of joy in our hearts, as we are gathered together with (_____ and _____) in the beauty of this church, surrounded by family and friends, as they come to speak their wedding vows.

It is our prayer they will always be blessed and united in the presence of God. That they will remember how precious they are to each other at this moment and will always be. That they may truly be happy and always sensitive and supportive of each other.

(_____ and _____), if you are ready, we will now gladly witness you join your hands, hear you pronounce your mutual promises, and envision the deep, God-inspired desire you have to be two in one.

James McKarns is pastor of St. Paul's Catholic Church, North Canton, Ohio.

14

Memory And Hope

For An Older Couple, Both Widowed

**Genesis 2:18-23; Psalm 100;
Colossians 3:12-17; John 15:9-12**

By Deborah D. Steed

The Bible contains many themes, but two of them that pervade both the Old and New Testaments are memory and hope. The Israelites were constantly reminded by their leaders and their religious rituals to keep uppermost in their minds the fact that God had saved them, had made them a nation, had bestowed on them through Abraham and Sarah a special covenantal love. This memory was recalled time and time again as Israel wandered through the centuries, as a way of calling a people back into that special relationship with God.

But they were not allowed to remain comfortable with memory alone. In fact, the prophets recalled these memories specially to engender hope that the nation could once again know the goodness of the Lord. Memory that they had been blessed, and hope that once again the hand of the Lord would rest upon them.

The early church, too, called forth memory and hope. The apostles, fresh from companionship with Jesus, recalled his physical presence before the ascension in order to gather strength and spread the gospel. And this memory compelled them to hope that once again they might enjoy that same union with him that they had had before his death. Memory gave them strength; hope gave them wings.

So it is with us today. Occasions such as your wedding are pivots upon which our memories and our hopes converge and turn together. You two bring the memories of your years together as well as some still fairly fresh memories of those decades before you knew one another. You bring the remembrance of your happy first marriages, families raised, your own children married, and grandchildren born. But you are not the only ones who bring memory to this occasion. We, your family and friends, bring them as well. We bring memories of you as children or teenagers, as our brother and sister, our parents and the spouses of our parents. And today those memories all come together for us.

We are not quite certain what to do with those memories, for they are dear to us still. We are not ready to discard them and yet we are loath to cling to them too closely, lest they hold us back from participating in your future.

Fortunately, we can look to the Bible for help. It is the biblical word that gives us permission to cherish those memories and to use them. For as the stories of the Israelites and the early church show us, God gives us our memories as a lasting treasure. They are dear to us as well as to God, for God is active in them. But God wants us to use them as a springboard into the future, as a surety against the divine promise: Lo, I am with you always.

You see, God never permits us to stand still in the present. Though we carry the past with us, we are always poised on the brink of tomorrow. We are always asked to be prepared for change, for that is the great and joyful surprise given us in creation. We are constantly called out of the comforts of what is the same into the challenge of what is new. And as we participate in new relationships, new opportunities, new events, we become co-creators with God, called to make something out of the surprise of life.

Perhaps this is the essence of grace: that we are never condemned to living on memory alone but are given the chance to transform our memory into living hope through the great promise inherent in our changing world. We are given the opportunity to take risks. We are challenged to embrace the world with joy.

So tonight we bring all our memories with us, and we present them as a gift to you: a gift that propels us into hope. It is a hope that out of the beauty and pain of your past, out of the uniqueness of this moment, God can fashion something new and good and lasting for our future as well as for yours. It is not only a hope that you will find deepest satisfaction in one another, but that this ungainly group that is now your new family — all of us with you tonight — that we will share in that happiness, that we will support you as husband and wife, that we will find great promise in your marriage. It is a hope that we can bring the best of ourselves to your relationship, that with God's help we can fashion out of what once seemed a static world something dynamic and filled with grace.

The psalmist says blessed are those who trust in the Lord. Tonight, as our memory and our hope converge in this celebration, we pray that together they meld into that kind of trust which allows God's blessings to shower down upon you and your marriage. May you love one another, may we love you, as Christ first loved us all. Amen.

Deborah D. Steed is associate pastor of Prince of Peace Lutheran Church, Loveland, Ohio.

15
Looking Outward Together

An Evening Service

1 John

By Warren Gregory Martin

(_____) I would like to take a few moments and speak with you and the congregation gathered to witness your covenant of marriage about the significance of what you do tonight. God has given you both a gift: the gift of love to share with each other and a relationship in which you have the trust and faithfulness of another. Each of those words — love and faithfulness — have a multitude of meanings for us, but the nature of this love and faithfulness you enter into through marriage carries with it a set of values of its own. Listen to what several people have written about love:

The writer of *The Little Prince*, Antione De Saint-Exupery wrote of love: "Love does not consist in gazing at each other, but in looking outward together in the same direction."

Elizabeth Barrett Browning: "How do I love thee? Let me count the ways. I love thee to the depth and breadth of height my soul can reach, when feeling out of sight for the ends of being and ideal grace. I love thee to the level of everyday's most quiet need, by sun and candlelight. I love thee freely, as men strive for right; I love thee purely, as they turn from praise. I love thee with the passion put to use in my old griefs, and with my childhood's faith. I love thee with a love I seemed to lose with my lost saints. I love thee with the breath, smiles, tears, of all my life! And if God choose, I shall but love thee better after death."

The apostle Paul said: "Love is patient, love is kind. It does not envy, it does not boast, it is not proud. It is not rude, it is not self-seeking, it is not easily angered, it keeps no record of wrongs. Love does not delight in evil but rejoices in the truth. It always protects, always trusts, always hopes, always perseveres. Love never fails."

The writer of 1 John: "This is love; not that we loved God, but that he loved us, and sent his Son as an atoning sacrifice for our sins. Dear friends, since God so loved us, we also ought to love one another."

And lastly, the words of Jesus: "As the Father has loved me, so have I loved you. Now remain in my love. If you obey my commandments, you will remain in my love, just as I have obeyed my Father's commands and remain in his love. I have told you this so that my joy may be in you and that your joy may be complete. My command is this: Love each other as I have loved you. Greater love has no one than this, that one lay down his life for his friend. You are my friends if you do what I command."

As you can plainly see, that which we celebrate today, the love you (_____) hold in your hearts for one another is many things. Poets and apostles and of course the Son of God have each spoken of the significance of love that is much more than an infatuation, or a desire that comes and goes. The love we command to you two today is the bond of your relationship which places demands upon you.

This love is after the fashion of the Heavenly Father for us: sacrificial, giving for the sake of another, not looking solely for what can be gained for yourself. It is the kind of love that has the power and experience to make up for the bad times and the wrongs we cross one another with. It is a love that brings two as yourselves to depend now upon one another.

And how does one come to the point of wanting to depend on another's care, but that there is an abiding trust. We have faith in God, whose promises are real. The veracity of that promise was revealed through the life, death and resurrection of God's own Son. In Jesus we have seen promise reach fulfillment. Your trust in one another is based on first believing in the goodness of each other, that your word and promise is sincere. And secondly, you each offer proof of the same, as you do what you will soon promise in your marriage vows.

When love waxes and wanes between the two of you, one thing abides. That is the promise of trust you have made to care for one another, to stand by one another, through the best and worst of what is to come. And in doing so, it is remarkable how the love becomes real once again. Strong faith doesn't come all at once. It is often gained through willing submission to love and goodness in the midst of trial. Let faithfulness be the mark of your love seen by others, that they might look upon this marriage made today, and give thanks for the beautiful witness it brings to them, and that it might be a model of what others will strive after.

Trust in the love and faith of your God who has given you this life together. Abide in God's presence and allow God's will and ways to guide you, and you will find it to be a great source of strength for you.

Let your life be the two of you looking together to a future, and what will be best for each in that tomorrow. You have some significant decisions to make about that future. Your labor of love will have to include each other in the process of deciding.

We give thanks to God for you and your love pledged here. God bless you and keep you in all the years ahead. Amen.

Warren Gregory Martin is pastor of Zion Evangelical Lutheran Church, Williamsport, Maryland.

16

Two Are Better Than One

Ecclesiastes 4:7-12

By Sandra Herrmann

Well, here we are — despite whatever trepidation you may have felt over the last few weeks or days, the time has finally arrived for you two to stand up before your family and friends and to announce your vows for everyone to hear. This is no small thing. In a world of change and uncertainty, when people move and change every aspect of their lives not once but three or four times in their lives, where the bonds of matrimony are easily severed when things go wrong, and every other marriage ends in divorce, you have decided to make some pretty serious promises.

First, you are promising that whatever happens, you will stick it out. Sickness, a failed business, long-term unemployment, a winning lottery ticket, a huge promotion, a sensation that you have "outgrown" your partner — none of these circumstances will give you an easy out. You will not shrug off your partner and "go on with your own life." You are declaring that "finding yourself" can happen within this relationship as easily as outside the bonds of marriage, that in fact you have found a part of yourself in finding this person standing beside you.

What you are declaring before your friends and family is that you have found a person you can trust, a person to whom you can turn when you hurt, when you're afraid, when you need comfort, and expect to be accepted. You are also declaring your willingness to be there for your partner when your partner needs to be accepted, forgiven, comforted and reassured.

These are not things easily accomplished. And it's a rare marriage where neither partner has ever done this.

For example, the day comes, as it must to every wife and mother, when the car is making some odd sound the mechanic claims he can't hear and the washing machine has taken to walking around the basement instead of getting the clothes clean, and your boss has told you you'll be working the next five Saturdays in a row, and just as the spaghetti boils over every burner on the stove your loving husband walks in and says, "Boy, have I had a lousy day! I hope supper's ready!"

Or, on the other hand, husbands — you've had one of those days where every car on the road seemed to be trying to occupy the exact space yours happens to be, and the first five people you talked to snapped at you, and halfway through an important meeting you discovered that the one piece of information you had to have seems to have disappeared. You're tired, the air conditioning in the car is apparently on strike, and when you go to freshen up you find the shower rod is strung with pantyhose.

It's moments like these that strain the vows you are about to take.

In fact, it's these moments that are more dangerous to a marriage than the major problems you may be called upon to face. We can usually pull together when the going gets tough; it's these "sandpiper" moments that can do us in, make us take out our discomfort on the one person we need in our lives.

Because, you see, the writer of Ecclesiastes really says it — our family, our spouses, our children, even our grandchildren, give our lives meaning. Our work means more than just going to the office or the factory, wherever we earn money. Our work becomes a means for providing a good home for our family, a future for our children. Whatever we put our hand to, it becomes a joint venture. We think not just of the task at hand, but how we are affecting the world our grandchildren will inherit. We are no longer alone, one powerless person in a world of chaos; we have become part of that endless chain, father to son, daughter to mother, a link between those who have gone before us to a future we cannot imagine.

You are no longer alone. Now, when one of you falls, there will indeed be someone to pick you up. There will always be someone to hold the ladder steady, to wake up in the middle of the night when you've heard a noise you can't identify. Always an eye to catch across the room, someone who remembers the same dumb joke and laughs at the same cartoons.

But more than that, you have the possibility of weaving that three-fold cord the preacher speaks of. You can beat the odds, and have the marriage that lasts a lifetime. And it's so easy: include God in your marriage.

You see, Jesus is the third cord that can make your marriage that strong lifeline that characterizes the very best marriages. And you can include him every day. Pray together, at least once a day. Morning or night, or before or after supper, take a few minutes. Read the scriptures. Just a small portion each day, it doesn't have to be much. One of the stories of Jesus, or one of the Psalms, or some story of the Old Testament. And then join your hands and your hearts together, and ask God to guide you, to teach you how to uphold one another. Ask God to bless your partner, and pray for the concerns of your partner. It only takes a few minutes each day, and it will make your marriage strong. You will have that unseen third partner to lean on, and you will grow strong as a result. You will find in time that you will be more accepting of your partner's foibles and shortcomings. It will be easier to forgive one another. And easier to admit you may have made a mistake, need to be forgiven, need to be comforted.

So, as you repeat the vows you are about to make, know that you do not have to struggle on your own to keep them. Include God in your daily married life as you are including God in this day, and you will be assisted every day to have a happy home and a long, loving life together. May God grant that this be so. Amen.

Sandra Herrmann is pastor of Faith United Methodist Church, Milwaukee, Wisconsin.

17

Congregation's Vow To The Couple

By Ann K. Larson

(May be read following vows, exchange of rings, declarations.)

Pastor *(to congregation):* And you, friends and family of
_____ and _____, you heard the commitment they
have made to each other. You are not here just to watch what
they are doing. You, too, participate in this marriage, by virtue of the love you have offered in the past, and by the same
which you will give in the future. So, I ask you now, do you
promise _____ and _____ your guidance, help, support and prayers in their life together. If so, answer "Yes, with
the help of God."

Response: Yes, with the help of God.

*(If you are the original purchaser of this material you have
permission to print this in a wedding bulletin for use as it was
intended.)*

Ann K. Larson, Bloomington, Indiana, is an interim pastor in the Indiana-Kentucky Synod of the ELCA.

18

Love Promises: The Eternal Dimension

Ephesians 5:21-22, 25

By Michael L. Thompson

As we gather here today for this festive occasion, Paul has some very good advice for _____ and _____ as they prepare to begin their life together. Paul writes:

> *Submit yourselves to one another out of reverence for Christ. Wives, submit yourselves to your husbands in the same way you submit to the Lord. Husbands, love your wives just as Christ loved the church and gave his life for it.* — Ephesians 5:21-22, 25

Paul had caught the vision of how relationships work best ... always showing concern for that other person's needs and wants ... loving that other person enough to listen and perhaps change to make things better. Paul knew from Christ's example that love in all its beauty has an eternal dimension which we can enjoy.

_____ and _____ are catching that same vision — discovering how beautiful it is to share dreams, to hear that other person's aspirations, to support each other through joys and sorrows, to submit themselves to one another — working together to make decisions which affect them both. They trust that their love for each other will be eternal.

After discovering the beauty of that kind of relationship, _____ and _____ have decided to commit themselves to God and to one another in a public way. In a few minutes they will make promises to one another and to God. And we are privileged to be here to listen in on those promises.

Those promises which they will make are among the most cherished gifts they will give to each other. We, too, have brought gifts for these two special people as we wish them well. But, I would suggest that a gift which they are giving to us, as we observe their promise-sharing, is the opportunity to examine our commitments to husbands, wives, children, parents, friends and our Lord.

_____ and _____ have put a lot of thought and prayer into their relationship, and they have taken this step toward commitment which is important. But we, in our relationships, find it easy at times to let those relationships slide for a time without any examination, or prayer, or renewal of promises.

What I would suggest is that today, you give all your interest and energy to celebrating with _____ and _____ as they move into a new and exciting relationship. But, tomorrow and the days following, let _____ and _____ promises to one another remind you to examine and renew your relationships with one another. Hopefully, your examination and renewal will be as celebrative and joy-filled as this wedding is.

Let us pray: Almighty God, we remember how the presence of your Son brought joy to a certain wedding at Cana in Galilee. We pray that you would use his eternal presence to sustain the joy of this wedding. Grant _____ and _____ the patience, courage, hope and love to state and live out their promises to you and to one another. Help us, as brothers and sisters in Christ, to be supportive of them in their new adventure together. In Jesus' name. Amen.

Michael L. Thompson, Findlay, Ohio, is a former pastor in the ELCA and is marketing associate of CSS Publishing Co.

19
Your Journey Of Life

For An Older Couple, Both Widowed

Ecclesiastes 4:9-12
1 Corinthians 13; John 15:9-12

By Mark P. Zacher

Family and friends of the bride and groom and especially you — _____ and _____ — on this your wedding day: Grace to you and peace from God our Father and from our Lord and Savior, Jesus Christ. Amen.

The journey of life for both of you has taken some rather unexpected turns and detours. The path and the road has perhaps not gone exactly the way that you planned a number of years ago. But, because of the rough spots and because of the turns and because of the detours, the paths of your lives have crossed and intersected. And, it is that, that crossing, that has brought you here before the altar of almighty God on this very special evening.

_____ and _____, you have come before this gathered assembly, before this altar of God, and into God's holy presence to enter into a deeper stage and commitment in your relationship. Before this company, before this altar, and before God, you will, in just a few moments, make vows of love to one another. And, they are holy vows and your action in sharing them speaks very powerfully to us about the reality of hope and about promise and above joy and about love.

I would like to, just briefly, remind you of some of the words that were read from the 13th chapter of Paul's first letter to the Corinthians. Paul wrote, "Love is patient and kind;

love is not jealous or boastful; it is not arrogant or rude. Love does not insist on its own way; it is not irritable or resentful; it does not rejoice at wrong, but rejoices in the right. Love bears all things, believes all things, hopes all things, endures all things. Love never ends; as for prophecies, they will pass away; as for tongues, they will cease; as for knowledge, it will pass away . . . (but) faith, hope, (and) love abide, these three, but the greatest of these is love.''

You know, perhaps a different translation of that last verse puts it into even stronger words. It reads: "In a word, there are three things that last forever: faith, hope, and love; but the greatest of them all is love.''

Now, I hope that all of you listened very, very closely and carefully as I reread that passage. You see, what we are being told by Paul is that no matter how the journey of life may go, no matter what the direction we may head, and no matter what rough spots and difficulties that we might endure; through it all we can be confident and hopeful and filled with joy because there are three things that are eternally sure and certain and that we can carry with us forever. There is faith and there is hope and there is love!

The faith of both of you is what has brought you through the difficult experiences that you have had. Your faith is what has enabled you to continue along the path of life, even when the road got difficult and the way got rough.

It was the hope of both of you that allowed your lives to intersect and to cross. And, it was that hope that allowed you to see a new day and a new life, together.

And, finally, it is your love that has brought you here together this evening. This day and this hour, this wedding and this union, are about love — love that can endure and love that can enrich both of you.

_____ and _____, I cannot help but to believe that it is because of your faith and your hope and your love that you have found one another. I cannot help but to believe that, through it all, this is what our heavenly Father wants so that you might be fulfilled and happy. And, I know that whatever the future brings, whatever unexpected twists and turns the journey of life might take you on, your faith and your hope and your love will endure and will carry you on — together!

My friends, _____ and _____, on this special day and in this special hour, may God richly bless you in the vows and the promises of love that you make. May God guide you and may he protect you. And, may you find and keep the joy of this moment with you forever — in your faith and with your hope and in your love. Amen.

Mark P. Zacher is associate pastor of Trinity Evangelical Lutheran Church, Camp Hill, Pennsylvania.

20
Inner Experience

By Mary Lu Warstler

Marriage requires generosity, unselfishness, flexibility, and forbearance from both husband and wife. The reality and happiness of your marriage depends upon the inner experience of your heart and the integrity of your commitment.

_____ and _____, today as you celebrate your marriage, you must realize that this ceremony is only an outward sign — a symbol for the world to know that your intention is to spend the rest of your lives together as husband and wife. There is no magic in a service like this. There are no special words that I can say that will make a marriage work.

The real marriage — the union of two lives — is a daily decision you must make as you determine to work through all the little trials and irritations of life, making that commitment to live each day of your lives in love and intimacy.

You are two separate individuals. You each have your own likes and dislikes, your hopes and dreams, your abilities and talents. That must never be lost in the togetherness. But there must be room for mutual enjoyments, hopes and dreams, and learning from one another. You are still two separate individuals, but you are now becoming one couple, uniquely joined together to become a family — sharing common goals seeking to share the rest of your lives each with the other.

You must continue to grow as individuals, but you must also grow as a family unit. Growth is sometimes painful. Each of you will find that you must give up something of your past in order for the future together to be as God intends it to be. Each new level of achievement will bring you closer together in love as you work together at growing in love and maturity.

Love is the key which unlocks the mysteries of relationships. God is love and therefore, all love is from God. Love is not just a "feeling" that we have. Love is a gift from God which must be nurtured and expressed in many ways. As love grows the surface feelings may change, but the deeper level of love will allow you to respond to one another as the apostle Paul speaks of love in his letter to the Corinthians.

He reminds us that love teaches us to be patient with one another — even when we disagree, even as we are learning all the moods and unexpected reactions and changes in each other. He teaches us that love instructs us to be kind to one another and not envy the other's talents and abilities. It is not selfish, seeking only to gratify our own needs and desires, but is self-giving, seeking to please the other and satisfy their needs and desires, while not giving up our own personhood.

We seek to be understanding and thoughtful, not being quick to take offense. Love does not keep score of all the wrongs, or imagined wrongs, but seeks always to reconcile and forgive.

Real love is from God and if you will ground your love for each other in that love of God, you will grow together. Marriage can not be a one-time commitment in a ceremony in the church. It must be a day-by-day growing, changing, learning, exploring, loving, hating, sharing of two unique individuals in a relationship which brings together male and female in God's plan for union, becoming one and yet remaining two.

Just as we cannot as individuals live in a vacuum by ourselves, no marriage is ever completely unaffected by the outside world. Friends and family have not only gathered here today to celebrate with you, but will be a source of help and strength, and yes, even disagreement in the years to come.

I would, therefore, charge you who witness and celebrate with _____ and _____ this happy occasion to continue to be a source of nurture and friendship in the years ahead. As God works together with _____ and _____ in binding them together with love, may he also work together with family and friends in bringing together a community of care and love.

Commitment is another key word for keeping alive the love you share this day. This ceremony is only a symbol. The real commitment and marriage takes place daily as you work together building a home in love and honor of God and each other.

Mary Lu Warstler is pastor of Kenmore United Methodist Church, Akron, Ohio.

21

You Are What You Wear

Song Of Solomon 8:6-7
Colossians 3:12-17

By Erskine White

From the announcement of their engagement to the day
of their wedding, a young couple can be put through an in-
credible amount of stress. A cynic might say that society intends this period as a kind of torture test to see if the couple
is really ready for the rigors of marriage. With the countless
decisions to be made and the numerous other people whose
interests and wishes must be accommodated, a young couple
needs the tact of a diplomat, the patience of a saint and the
endurance of a marathon runner when preparing for their wedding day.

_____ and _____, I congratulate you on hav-
ing passed this torture test. I congratulate you for surmount-
ing all the hurdles and hassles which presented themselves in
recent weeks and months, and for navigating your way to this
time and place, where you are now ready to be joined together
in the sight of God.

One part of this extended text which must be endured before a wedding day is that everyone and his cousin must give
you advice. Of course, this advice can be eminently memora-
ble or entirely forgettable, but there is something to be said
for the urge to give it. The truth is that a young couple just
getting married has a lot to learn about love. The truth is that
every married couple always has a lot to learn about love, no
matter how many wedding anniversaries they have celebrated
together.

When we speak of love, we speak not of sentiment or passion, but of the depths and mysteries of life. When we speak of marriage, we speak not of a product but a process. Marriage has been ordained by God for many purposes, and one of them is to provide us a place where we may learn to be fully human, since we are fully human when we fully love.

What kind of advice have people given you in recent months? Perhaps some have talked to you about the importance of communication in a marriage. Honest, open talk. The kind of communication where your spouse is the one person who shares your deepest hopes, knows your deepest fears and understands your deepest needs.

Take time with each other, and do not think that avoiding certain topics is the way to keep peace in a marriage. This is a mistake too many couples make. They find they cannot talk about the children without arguing, so they stop talking about the children. They find they cannot talk about money or sex or relations with the in-laws without arguing, so they agree not to talk about money or sex or relations with the in-laws. They keep adding difficult topics to the list of things they won't talk about until one day, they wake up and discover they cannot talk about anything! Their marriage has died. It is far better to learn right from the beginning how to talk about uncomfortable subjects.

Maybe some of your advice-giving friends have talked to you about various other hazards of married life, like the dangers of self-centeredness, the threat of complacency, or any of a hundred other problems to be avoided at all costs in your life together. I suppose that advice is useful enough, but it doesn't get to the heart of the matter, does it. It doesn't address the most critical question you need to face together, which is — what are you going to wear once you are married? That's right: I woke up this morning with my mind set on fashion! In fact, my advice to you can be summed up in five words: you are what you wear.

Actually, it's not my advice, but God's, spoken through his apostle, Paul, so I can give it to you with complete confidence. Paul writes this about what you should wear:

Put on then, as God's chosen ones, holy and beloved, compassion, kindness, meekness and patience, forbearing one another and, if one has a complaint against the other, forgiving each other; as the Lord has forgiven you, so you must also forgive. And above all these, put on love, which binds everything together in perfect harmony. And let the peace of Christ rule in your hearts . . .

When you look in your closet and wonder what you will wear, remember Paul. Put on the undergarments of compassion, and the shirt of kindness. Put on the pants of lowliness, the belt of meekness and the stockings of patience. And remember what Paul says about forgiveness. When you go to the closet to select a pair of shoes, put on the shoes of forgiveness, for if there is one thing you can be certain of as you build your future together, it is that there will be occasions when both of you will have to forgive and be forgiven.

When you have put on all this clothing, put on the coat of love, which binds everything together in perfect harmony. It is the perfect accessory for every occasion, this coat of love, and its fabric is made from the life and witness of Jesus Christ, who is the way, the truth and the life. Let the peace of Christ rule in your hearts, and you will learn everything you need to know about love in the years ahead.

Right now, your love comes easily to you. It is new and exciting. You know the emotions and desires the ancient Israelites knew when they sang at their own weddings: "Set me as a seal upon your heart, as a seal upon your arm . . ."

But you will not always be young, and your love will not always be easy. You will have to learn to cope as a couple with the joys and sorrows life can bring. Through it all, you will not be able to control the circumstances which shall affect your life together, but you can control the way you look, so pay attention to the dress code in your marriage. Look in the mirror each day and see what you are wearing. Put on the kindness, the consideration, the forgiveness and love which can conquer even the severest of life's trials and tribulations. You are what you wear, and with the way the two of you feel about each other today, I know you will always want to be wearing your very best.

Erskine White is a chaplain to the Asheville School, Asheville, North Carolina.